Get Up, Get Dressed and Get Out the Door

Your guide to getting unstuck from your usual routine, getting back to basics, and taking your business to the next level.

by Jean MacDonald, DTM

Published by:
Alphagraphics
Vernon Hills, IL
847-816-7373
www.us278.alphagraphics.com

Graphic Design by:
Koch Creative Services, Inc.
www.kochcreative.com

Photography by:
Jonathan's Portraits
847-821-1700
www.jonathansportraits.com

First Edition publication date September 2012

ISBN 978-0-9883022-1-1

If you are unable to order this book from your local bookseller, you may order
through www.NetworkConnectSucceed.com or jeanconnects@gmail.com.

Dedication

*Thank you Mom for raising me with
the "Get up, Get Dressed, Get out the Door" attitude.
Mom was a woman beautiful inside and out.
She taught me the most valuable lessons.
Integrity, confidence, image, manners and
always having an attitude of gratitude. She passed when I was
a young woman but left memories that are priceless.
Thank you, Mom! I love you!*

Contents

Acknowledgements

This book has taken me a long time to get out the door. I hope that you will enjoy reading the basics of getting yourself unstuck.

Several people are responsible for this book being published, and I want to thank all of them for taking the time to make this possible. It is their wisdom that will help so many as they go through their days and have those "stuck" moments.

Thank you to all of these very special people:

Susan Carson, Ph.D. - Friends for over 20 years, my coach and mentor for several years. Thank you for always listening with an open mind and heart.

Phillip Gafka - An extraordinary Executive Business Coach. Helping me with goals, leadership and skills, he is the best.

Libby Kozak - She is the best of the best and has been my business consultant and assistant for several years. Keeping me in line and always looking great in print.

Beverly McKeen - What a joy to work with at Toastmasters and mentoring in professional speaking.

Laura Risi - My beautiful daughter who has helped me in so many ways and is always there for me.

Derek Schoch - My son, friend, mentor and joy in my life. Thank you for your encouragement.

Kristen Schoch - A very special daughter-in-law who I love working with.

Nicki Schuh - Friend, master marketing consultant and a true listener.

To those that made the book come together:

Aaron Risi - My son and extraordinary artist. Thank you for sharing your talent.

Tim Schoch - My editor and friend, thank you for all the rewrites and great insight to make this come together.

Christie Sweatman - Your help through the publishing process was priceless. Thank you for bringing my vision to life.

Introduction

I enjoy helping people find a direction, giving a road map with a vision for success. You rarely can motivate anyone, but you can inspire someone to be the best they can be and give them tools to help make the journey easier.

It is said, "If no one knows you, how can they do business with you?" Getting out the door is the one basic thing that anyone who wants to achieve anything must do.

The Naked Salesman

You can't run out the door naked, without protection, without a direction and without tools. You can't expect to get out of a rut or achieve your goals without preparation.

Before you even think about turning the doorknob, you have to wake yourself up, prepare an image that will make a great impression, and make a plan that will give you results…so when you do finally step through that doorway, the world for you is full of nothing but possibilities…. opportunities that you are prepared for.

I wrote this book to help you Get Up, Get Dressed, and Get Out the Door. Lastly, get the results you are aiming for.

The Economy: Adjusting to Sell

Everybody knows that we go through cycles all the time in business. When times are good, it's easy to fall into the trap of getting too comfortable. Can we expect the customer to keep ordering and buying in bad times as they have in good times? I'll answer that: No.

I remember reading a recent Wall Street Journal article about when the economy changes we must change our business thinking, as well. The article said that those that do this are the ones who can become the leading businesses of the future by possessing four things:

1.   A quality product
2.   A product sold at a fair price
3.   Inventory to support it
4.   Extraordinary customer service

Networking, Networking, Networking

So, now that you are properly dressed and prepared, and now that you have a realistic view of the economy, what now?

Now, it is vital for salespeople and business owners to not only open that door, but be visible all the time.

This is difficult for some to understand, much less achieve, because they do not grasp the power of networking and following up—and how enjoyable it can be.

I love to talk to people and understand who they know, where they are from and how I can connect them.

→ Remember: It is far, far easier to maintain a solid relationship with a customer or prospect than it is to go out into the cold and chase down new business. You can bank on it.

◧ The Door Opener

There are many books on sales techniques, time management and building connections. I wanted to write something a little different about how to get "unstuck." This book can help you get out the door, believe that you can get results, adjust to the current economic climate, and get your name and face out the door every day to get your business flowing and keep it growing.

What's holding you back, tripping you up, blocking your path? Let's identify those things, get your hand on the doorknob, and fling open that door.

In this book, you'll find a great deal of hands-on, smart advice from my own experience and what I've learned from others. Everyone who contributed to this book has weathered business storms and emerged healthier and more successful.

At the end of each chapter I have left a thought or question that you can use to help you "get unstuck." There are pages for your thoughts and revelations. I would love to hear from you.

This book is yours to be used not just read. There are very simple solutions for getting the achievements you want. Go back to the basics and watch what happens!

On one hand, this book is personal. On the other, it is strictly business. I think this formula will help you bounce back faster.

Remember, we can all get stuck and have ups and downs in business. It is how fast we recover that makes the difference.

Read this book and refer to it often to find your gems of wisdom, or what I call the Diamonds on the ground. Believe me, they are there.

Enjoy----and good luck!

Jean MacDonald

It's a Jungle Out There
It's a jungle out there -- or is it?

How can some have such a clear path and see where their next deal or connection is coming from, but others have such a difficult time getting out of their own way?

Excuses hold us back, or fear...fear of taking a chance, or fear of the unknown. Yes, the journey can be tough when there is no vision or a poor attitude. Then, we fear what might pop out of those jungles or what will be around the next bend.

Take time to venture into the jungle and learn all you can. Only then can you hack through the blind doubt and take advantage of the golden opportunities.

What jungle did you venture into recently -- and how did you successfully find your way out?

Did you have great success in the jungle, so you felt you could conquer anything that came in your way?

Did you meet the new connection and make the sale that led you to a new refreshing relationship?

Remember these successes and victories, then take that same scenario and do it again. I bet it will lead to better paths and more exciting ways to help you build your business.

Nothing ventured, nothing gained, nothing to draw on the next time.

Door Opener

After answering the questions in the chapter, reflect on those answers and see how you can develop new vision!

Chapter 2

Get out of that Slump FAST!

Bounce back ability! We all have lows and highs in business. Recovery is key, and what we are doing to recover quicker so business does not flounder is important. I was taught several years ago when I was in a slump to STOP everything, take my mind off what was happening and do something for myself. In other words, get my mind off the problem.

The old adage is we are going to hit the wall at some time. We are going through a crisis, in a crisis, or coming out of one. They happen to all of us in business and in life.

Do you constantly beat up on yourself or make excuses why things are not working? This is setting yourself up for disastrous results.

Do you want to wake up next year where you are today, or are you willing to take action and stop procrastinating? Do you notice how successful people just seem to keep on going, seem to always make the next sale, land the next deal?

-STOP- You can also have the same success!! They have just learned to bounce back faster. When they do have the valleys of business they regroup, look at the situation, find mentoring help and move on. They don't hash it over and over or use the woulda, coulda, shoulda!

Here are some basics that could help you out of this SLUMP:

1. **STOP!** Break the cycle, do something else and get your mind off the present situation.

2. **Go back to the Basics.** It has been said by many great sales leaders that going back to the basics of the business will help you develop your skill level and generate business faster. The basics are learning the script, teaching technique or understanding how to deal with the customer. Go back and learn these simple skills.

3. **Focus** on what you have done well in the past and do this again. Look back at the things that have made you successful and work on those again.

4. **Stop Criticizing** what you shoulda, woulda, coulda. You can do it and you need to believe and be kind to yourself.

5. **Don't compete with others!** This is your game and your journey. Think about how to do better yourself. Focus on today and have the best day ever.

6. **Don't make major decisions** when you are in this mood. Our judgment may not be clear when we are in this Slump. The approach is to reassess your situation and move forward.

Door Opener

Take the time to reevaluate your slump! What are the basic things you can do that will move you forward? What have you done for you lately? It is not all about work. Find the balance that will give you the energy to move in the right direction.

Marketing U
What separates U from YOUR competition?

Marketing U begins with Knowing U. If nobody knows you, how can they do business with you? Getting out the door is vital.

I have moved several times making me the new kid on the block over and over again. To build my business I've had to get out the door and get involved in the community.

I have lived in my current location for nine years and I bet I know more people than those who have lived here all their lives.

I make it my business to be involved.

Get Out in the Marketplace

Do you spend a lot of time meeting people or placing ads expecting results? Nothing beats getting out there, meeting people and building connections.

I have been involved in several organizations that are national and international. These are very effective for growth, if you are willing to spend the time and do the legwork.

Ask, Then Listen

People love to talk about themselves. Let them. You never know what gold they will reveal.

YES, it takes time. But without getting to know others who know people you may want to know, how do you expect to grow your business? In the back of the book are several resources that can help you build your business.

Give to Receive

Besides getting out there and meeting the people, remember we must help others get what they want so you receive in return. This is an attitude of gratitude. People will do business with you if they like, know and trust you, but also if you can help them find connections without expecting anything in return.

Here's Looking at You

Let's talk about your image. Here's one that really makes my hair curl: dress-down Friday. Is looking like a day at the ball park or out on the farm doing chores helpful to your sales image or business?

Dress-down Friday has turned into I-don't-know Thursday, roll-out-of-bed Wednesday, I-am-not-sure Tuesday to I-don't-care Monday.

I am not saying being in a business suit is always the best dress, but looking like you care can certainly help you feel better and be ready for anything.

Mother's wise advice:
"Always be ready for the next opportunity."
(And she wasn't talking about groceries.)

I remember, it was a Friday because we had dress-down day at the company where I worked. I was not in dress-down mode, which is why I was chosen to go on an account for a large trucking company that called that morning. Others in the office (in their jeans) were annoyed because I was the new kid on the block.

I learned two things that morning. One: Always be ready to go out the door for the sale. Two: Mom was right and I will never forget what she taught me.

By the way, I did write that account and that customer remained in our office for over 10 years.

Attitude Can Make or Break You

To go along with marketing U, how well do you know your product or service? Are you arrogant, timid or plesantly assertive?

Years ago when I was a salesperson in the insurance business, arrogant agents couldn't understand why they would write the business but did not retain it. Their know-it-all attitude put the damper on some of the gatekeepers at different businesses. If they really knew it all, they'd remember that those gatekeepers can make or break them, and then make the necessary attitude adjustments.

I always respected the women at the front desk, and the women who worked for the executives. Being in their shoes before being in sales reminded me of how I always wanted to be treated. This helped me retain the business and also built a trust that became a factor when asking for referrals and having a long-term relationship.

On the other hand, if your attitude is timid, this can send out mixed emotions to the buyer and possibly lose the sale.

Solution: Know your product and be confident. If there is a question you cannot answer, be truthful and let them know you will get the answer. This builds credibility and trust with the buyer, and it makes you look good.

Door Opener

What are you doing to separate yourself? Attitude, image, product knowledge, being visible, building relationships and being affiliated in organizations. Marketing U can really be rewarding!

_____

_____

_____

_____

_____

_____

_____

_____

_____

_____

_____

_____

_____

_____

_____

_____

_____

_____

_____

_____

_____

_____

Turning Obstacles into Opportunities!
By Beverly McKeen

Some say getting started is the hardest. My experience told me that that's not necessarily true for everyone.

When writing my book, "MudPies & ButterFlies," the creative juices would come to a halt and I would find myself staring at a blank computer screen. The harder I would try to find the right words, the harder it would be to capture them.

I would ask myself; "Can I really do this? Why is it such a struggle if this were meant to be? Maybe I'm shooting too high."

This was the kind of "negative" self talk that would play over and over in my head.

That's when I would sit back in my chair, close my eyes, and meditate for however long it took until I felt a sense of peace, a sense of knowing.

I needed to connect to something/someone more powerful than me to remind myself why I felt called to write my message in the first place. It escaped me that my Higher Power was there to guide me. I didn't have to do this alone. This helped me tremendously with shaking those anxious moments of self doubt.

You see, we often get in our own way when seeking our purpose, our dreams and goals.

Yes, we have goals and dreams for ourselves, and that's a good thing. More often than not these dreams or goals are a reflection of our gifts that have manifested through our desire to tap into our authentic self. It is this desire that is the driving force that will often motivate us to take action.

Gifts are just that: a blessing that we should not turn our back on. So what do we do with these gifts? We develop them, we nurture them, and then share them with the world.

We have to remind ourselves that not only will we benefit by this, but more importantly…

By celebrating our accomplishments, we give others permission to do the same.

So when we lose sight of this, we can get stuck as we face one obstacle after another. Getting stuck often makes us lose our motivation to move forward.

It's during this difficult phase that most people give up.

Did you ever think that maybe these obstacles are opportunities that will help guide us in the right direction?

Again, when writing my book, I often found that when I was on the wrong track, nothing seemed to fit. It was like I was forcing the round pieces of the puzzle to fit in the square shapes.

Forcing it just doesn't work.

Letting go of any expectations and just simply allowing it to happen will give you the results that will bring you the greatest satisfaction. Ask your Higher Power to put the right people in your path that will help you realize your goals, your dreams. Then pay close attention to the people who suddenly surface in your life. They are there to help you just as you are meant to be in their life for whatever reason.

So often, we think our journeys are ours to experience alone. But I learned that wasn't so. We are all part of one another's journey and each of us plays a significant role in each other's quest.

Once I was able to put my mind around that, it seemed I was more open to receive new ideas and no longer felt that I was swimming against the current. The current would now carry me to the next place and the next and the next. That's quite an accomplishment for an "A" type personality!

Before my journey began, I would figuratively kick doors open to get results, anything that would bring me instant results. But these results were not long lasting. Nothing seemed to work.

It was then that I learned not all doors were meant to open for me.

Those that were seemed to open with ease and grace, inviting me to walk through them, free of fear and doubt. I relinquished my need to be in control of things. It was a matter of trust. Letting go and having faith.

It was a huge relief to know that I didn't have to have all the answers.

Just being mindful to take some form of action daily, no matter how small, would soon find things evolving as they should. This time, I would "allow" the words to flow freely from my "heart" onto the paper.

So often we rely only on the thinking process to find our answers when what we really need is to tap into our hearts.

When we think things through without letting our emotions in, we often lose that soulful part of us. Once we can get in touch with our most inner "being," the doing part is no longer a struggle.

If you're facing obstacles and things seem to be getting in your way of realizing your dreams and your goals, take a moment to find that quiet place within and embrace the silence so your heart is open to receive. Then give yourself permission to receive all the blessings that await you. Continue to feed your desires as you connect with your authentic self.

Put your best intentions out there and let go. Believe, trust, and allow yourself to have what it is you desire.

What greater gift can you give to yourself and to the world? Do what makes your heart happy. It's speaking to you for a reason.

Door Opener

What is your desire? Do you take the time to STOP and listen to yourself? What are you doing today that will help move you forward?

_____

_____

_____

_____

_____

_____

_____

_____

_____

_____

_____

_____

_____

_____

_____

_____

_____

_____

_____

_____

_____

Chapter 5

Attitude
By Phillip Gafka, CBC

One of my most memorable childhood lessons I learned from my mother. She had the wisdom to teach me and my siblings that we always had a choice.

When it was time for chores, like sweeping the stairs, washing the dishes or yard work, Mom always told us we had a choice – we (a) could do it and like it or (b) do it and not like it…but we *were* going to do it.

Our attitude is what we do with choices, and attitude is everything.

You have heard it before and it is as true today as the first time you heard it: Attitude is more important than what you do, because it affects how well you do everything.

There is no challenge in identifying the people with attitude. We can spot the person with the winning attitude or the one with the competitive attitude and we can easily spot the people with the poor or negative attitude.

Beyond these stereotypical attitudes in people that we encounter every day, there are people that exhibit less definable attitudes, but they have them just the same.

So what are these other attitudes that have so much influence in and over our lives? Our perceptions, insights, opinions, mental sets, the manner of how we act and feel, and our dispositions are just a few descriptors.

If we can recognize that our skills are the "how" we do something and our knowledge is the "what" we do, then we can identify that attitudes are the "why" we want to do something. The "why" is a far more powerful influencer than "how" or "what."

Chapter 5

Attitudes are habits of thought and they impact everything we do.

The way we think impacts the way we behave and the way we behave impacts what we do and how well we do it.

Where do our attitudes come from?

Behavioral psychologists have determined that the overwhelming majority of our attitudes, some say up to 95%, were developed by the time we were five years old.

Think about what we were learning at that early age. We were learning how to be socialized and protected. Our parents and the other adult influencers in our lives at that time were doing their best to give us a solid foundation to grow into young adults and be responsible citizens.

Unfortunately, much of the early influence that was bestowed upon us was from a negative perspective, as we were taught all the behaviors that we should <u>not</u> engage in.

You remember the time honored "Don't talk to strangers, Don't speak unless spoken to and Don't go where we're not wanted." So many rules and so many things not to do!

With a bit more understanding of what attitudes are and where they emanate from, what do we actually do with them? In other words, how do we assimilate our attitudes into our daily life?

The real magic of attitudes is in the way we make them work for us. A long term attitude of success may very well translate into a strong work ethic and the discipline to get out of bed each morning with an intention to achieve our short and long term goals. That same attitude may also include elements of the way we pace our lives and the degree of intensity which we apply to our efforts.

We cannot run full-out every day and then be refreshed enough to do it again tomorrow.

There is a certain pace of life that demands that we understand the "gas-brakes" effect.

Thinking that we can (or should) run as fast as we can every day is a prescription for disaster. A positive attitude about life, our dreams, goals and expectations must encompass a healthy dose of practicality: a plan for how we are to accomplish all the things we set out to do.

The "gas-brakes" concept is fundamental to achieving a long, healthy, successful and happy existence.

Whether setting the bar for ourselves or the people who report to us, we must have an understanding of how the things in our lives actually fit together. Since we cannot possibly accomplish everything in one day, we need to know how far we can push ourselves, and others, towards our defined goals.

To explain it in another way, observe the winning habits of your favorite professional sports athlete. Regardless of who they are, they do not play "all out" for the entire game or match.
Going into a game they have no idea of how that game will progress, but they instinctively know when they have to give everything they have during the competition.

They may have to perform at a maximum level only twice per game or as many as a dozen or more. What makes them the top professionals in their chosen sport is their talent and attitude and the way they apply it. Incorporating that concept into our everyday lives is what hard work and success are all about.

The "gas" part is our hard work and perseverance and the "brakes" part is the time spent actually enjoying the fruits of our labors, our relationships with loves ones and friends, as well as the quality of life that we have worked so hard for.

Our attitudes are also the way we view the world and how it affects us.

It has been said that we cannot control what happens to us, but we can control how we deal with it. We will all have a few curve balls thrown our way over the course of our lives, some more challenging than others, but we all get them. The fact is our attitudes help us navigate through these challenges to get to the other side.

For all intents and purposes we do get to the other side, but most importantly it is how we position ourselves for the journey through our challenges -- with gritty determination that somehow, someway we will get through whatever life throws at us.

We can do this from a positive perspective or a negative one, the choice is ours.

And we do have a choice, just as my mother counseled. Her instructions included the caveat that we could do something and like it or do something and not like it – but we were going to do it. The choice of how we did it was ours to make, just as it is yours.

Door Opener

What is your attitude when you are challenged? How do
you work through these challenges?

_____

_____

_____

_____

_____

_____

_____

_____

_____

_____

_____

_____

_____

_____

_____

_____

_____

_____

_____

_____

_____

_____

_____

Meet FRANK
Who do you know and how well do they know you?
Let's talk FRANK.

Friends, Relatives, Associates, Neighbors, Kids

This is a Basics 101. When we get stuck we need to go back to the basics and find that missing link that could help you get to your next connection or referral. FRANK can help you.

It is the simple things that we overlook that could be the key to our next success.

I remember talking to one of the women on my team about how she was really stuck, not sure who to call or what to do next to move her business forward. I said to her, "Get a FRANK sheet out and let's look at who you know."

I got a little snicker when I mentioned this sheet, since she is an experienced consultant. She pulled FRANK out of her file and we started looking at who would come to mind.

Immediately she said, "I found the missing link." She was so excited and told me she needed to get on the phone right away.

I asked what it was she saw in the FRANK sheet. She said, "I am on the alumni committee for my sorority from college and there are several hundred women I can contact and many locally that I have done business with."

Going back to the basics was the key.

I am amazed at how many people I sit down with that are "stuck." They are not sure who to contact or are not willing to get out the door to make things happen, maybe because they don't know where to look.

Looking inside your customer base is the first key to that success.

Those that love your products or services are the first clue. Pick five of those people, call and let them rave about you. You will feel great to begin with, but then ask who they can refer you to.

Download a full-sized version from my website www.NetworkConnectSucceed.com

FRANK
Contact List

Create a name list with the help of FRANK. Creating a list of contacts will help you get your business started. As your business grows, add new names and continue to use it to build your business.

Friends	Relatives	Acquaintances	Neighbors	Kids
• Grammar School	• Parents	• Doctor/dentist	• Present	• Girl Scouts
• High School	• In-laws	• Bank employees	• Past	• Cub Scouts
• College	• Grandparents	• Wait staff	• Parents of	• Nursery school
• Business	• Siblings	• Delivery staff	neighbors	parents
• Past employment	• Aunts/Uncles	• Postal employees	• Friends of	• Teachers
• Religious	• Cousins	• Hair dresser	neighbors	• PTA groups
organizations	• Relatives' friends	• Child care	• Relatives of	• School bus driver
• Social	• Godparents	• Health club	neighbors	• Athletic coaches
organizations		• Real estate		• Crossing guards
		• Insurance		• Activities:
		• Grocery store		dancing, piano,
				sports

For more information contact
Jean MacDonald
847-816-6764 / 413-222-7250
jeanconnects@gmail.com
www.NetworkConnectSucceed.com

Door Opener

Who do you know? Make a list of all of your friends, relatives, acquaintances, neighbors, and people your kids know. Use the previous page to help you build your list. Be FRANK with yourself and see what happens!

Organization 101

There have been many studies, but I think it is reliable to state that when you repeat something for 21 days it becomes a habit.

What does this mean to you as a businessperson? It means that one of your goals should be to find the best practices for you and keep doing them until they become part of how you run your enterprise.

Sticking with a plan can be the best habit you could ever create. In fact, make it an addiction.

As part of our road map to success, having a starting point and a plan each week and each day will get you out the door and develop new contacts. **A calendar, whether paper or mobile, is necessary.**

Note: Keep in mind if you have more than one business, have only one form of calendar. This is important since trying to track with two different calendars will make it more confusing.

I also recommend that you have a daily to-do sheet, in conjunction with your weekly plan. Having both a weekly plan that you develop every Sunday and a daily to-do sheet will help you feel more organized and improve your success rate as you collect leads and go to different events.

Here are some personal tips that have helped me organize my week, fill my date book and keep business flowing without loss of information.

1) **Color Your World:** I highlight my week with different colors: green for business, yellow for personal and family time including doctor appointments and date night, and pink for a second business that can be weaved in.

2) **Local Events Invite Conversations:** I go through the local papers, meet ups, and other internet resources to see what is going on in the community. This helps me find places to network and meet new referral sources. These are great places to practice meeting others and improve your comfort level.

3) **Dealing with 52 Pick-up:** What to do with all those contacts and business cards? I use an application to scan them and categorize them. I also use another internet program to send contacts and customers a written card.

4) **Never Forget a Follow-up:** I carry a notebook that I date for the month. As I meet people or take calls everything goes in this notebook. I date it on each page as I meet someone and I use it for my follow-up. At the end of the month I go through each page to see what needs to be followed up, and if it is complete I run a line through the page denoting that it is complete. If there are things that are incomplete I move them to the beginning of the new book and make sure I complete them within the first week of the new month. The old book then gets saved on a shelf for about 6 months and tossed after that.

These are some simple beginnings from my repertoire of best practices that you can implement right now into your day.

Door Opener

What systems do you have in place that are simple and can help you get out the door?

Networking Doesn't Work.
Practice with a Purpose Does!

I recently attended a large networking function and was totally amazed at the number of business cards being passed. It was speed networking, moving from table to table, giving a 60-second elevator speech and then handing out cards to everyone at the table.

Speed networking is a question of quantity vs. quality.

Most people seemed so excited to receive so many cards.

"Wow," one guy said to me, "I have gotten 67 cards today."

To his amazement, I said, "How many are you going to follow up with for a cup of coffee?"

I wasn't trying to be a smart aleck, but what will 67 business cards from one event get you but a mountain of cards for your desk!

Networking and time are often not partners. Networking doesn't work if you can't meet with new contacts right away. In two weeks, they won't remember who you are or what you did.

Think of following up with someone, not as something to do later, but as continuing a conversation.

Wouldn't it make more sense to go to an event with a goal in mind?

Why not set up a meeting with 2 or 3 people that have the same enthusiasm as yourself? Set up a cup of coffee, and see if there is synergy between the two of you. If there is, start to establish a relationship that could help both of you.

Let's look at the real definition of networking. I like to call it **"Vision Casting"** – helping others through my connections, customers, organizations, family and friends to find business. Mutual relationships that benefit both parties are the ONLY fruitful relationships.

Networking that Will Work for You

Misconceptions about Networking
1. Not a numbers game; relationship building
2. Not who you know but how well you know them
3. More than 60 seconds to connect; farming not hunting

Easy Ways to Improve Your Results
1. Plan
2. Don't sell — Listen
3. Help others get what they want

The key to networking is
**Showing Up and
Being Memorable**

Increase your effectiveness at networking events:

Before
☆ Have a purpose
☆ Bring a guest
☆ Be selective about events to attend

During
☆ Arrive early
☆ Behave like a host
☆ Introduce people to each other

After
☆ Follow up with contacts
☆ Invite to other events
☆ Make connections

<u>Business Building Coffee Conversation</u>

Creating Connection
1. Tell me a little bit about yourself
2. What do you enjoy most about what you do?
3. Where do you see yourself in the next 5 years?
4. Things we have in common

Developing Relationship
1. Biggest challenge?
2. How can I help you grow your business?
3. Who can I introduce you to?
4. Let me tell you about the organizations I belong to

Network ✕ Connect ✕ Succeed™
Helping you achieve your maximum potential

*For more information contact
Jean MacDonald
847-816-6764 / 413-222-7250
jeanconnects@gmail.com
www.NetworkConnectSucceed.com*

Copyright 2012, by Jean MacDonald

Chapter 8

Door Opener

Make a list of people with whom you need to follow up.
Reach out and get the "conversation" started.

Meeting Once is Nice, Twice is Great, Building Relationships is Priceless!

It is just amazing when you meet with someone for coffee to discuss mutual business and the conversation is all about them. It seems that no business gets discussed and you leave the table empty-handed.

The next thing I hear is the other person never gives any referrals. Time and again I hear this. People come to me complaining about so-and-so never giving referrals or leads. They get all the referrals because it is easy to refer to them, but why don't they give any referrals?

The realization is maybe they don't know HOW! Maybe you didn't ask in the right way. Don't expect them to refer themselves, maybe ask who do they know. Educate them with a story of success you have had in the past. Paint a clear picture of what or who you want to be connected with.

Are you amazed that your phone does not ring?

Do you wonder why people are not calling asking you for advice or referrals? Maybe they don't know how to ask, or they think that you really are not a very good source for connections.

Are you that complainer that is looking but never volunteers to help? Are you out in the community making a difference, or are you sitting in your office waiting for the phone to ring, waiting for that next referral to just pop in your office?

Get up, get dressed and get out and set up those cups of coffee. See who you can help today.

In the pages that follow is a list of questions that has helped me identify how to look for business for others. Study this list, practice it, make it yours.

Also, I always carry a spiral notebook. In it, I date when I met a person, take notes about them and what they are looking for. Then I send them an e-mail to let them know I will make the connections or possibly refer them to someone in the same field that may be able to help.

Networking is like golf -- 10% really get it and are good at it. Like golf, you need to practice. Sometimes in golf you will hit a great shot that makes you feel so good, and sometimes with networking you can really help someone else if you are willing to listen.

Listen, reach out and help, then find the key that connects you to the leads and referrals.

Does this take time and effort? You bet it is time-consuming. But think of all the wonderful people you are meeting and all the credibility that you are developing for yourself.

The more you give, the more abundance you will receive.

This is not just money, but terrific friends, heartfelt notes of appreciation and so much more.

Questions to Ask at a Business Building Interview

Below are some excellent starter questions for breaking the ice and doing some fruitful fishing for prospects. These questions will help you bond with a prospect and expand your network.

Add your own questions if you like, to expand the experience into other mutual areas you might discover with people.

A great exercise is to honestly answer the questions below. This will help you understand yourself as a businessperson.

So, first, take a few minutes to interview yourself. Don't respond with answers you feel business partners might like to hear. Instead, answer honestly and frankly.

1. Relationship building questions

a) What do you enjoy most about what you do?

_____

_____

b) How did you get in your current business or position?

_____

_____

c) What are some things we have in common?

_____

_____

d) Tell me a little about your family.

_____

_____

2. Trust building questions

a) What is your biggest challenge?

_____

_____

b) What is your biggest challenge...really? (You'll be surprised at how the answers change when you repeat this question with a bit more urgency)

_____

_____

3. Connection building questions

a) How can I help you grow your business?

_____

_____

b) Who can I introduce you to?

_____

_____

c) Let me tell you about the organizations and associations I belong to.

_____

_____

Other questions that occurred to you:

_____

_____

_____

_____

_____

_____

_____

_____

_____

_____

_____

_____

_____

Door Opener

Look at the Business Building Questions, set up a cup of coffee and see how you can open doors!

Stuck on TIME?
Here's the way out!
By Philip Gafka, CBC

Is this you?

There aren't many people today not challenged in some way by time, i.e., "I don't have enough time to get it all done" and "Where does the time go?" and so on.

So where does the time go?

Usually it is wasted or frittered away doing "busy" work or trying to look busy—or flat-out doing the wrong things. Spinning your wheels all day long isn't going to help you get out of life (or business) what you're expecting.

To more effectively manage your time, first figure out what you're trying to accomplish with your life and career.

When you have a clear idea of where you're trying to go, it's much easier to get there—and arrive on time!

A quick and simple tactic.

To help you begin managing your time right away, utilize some type of daily planning system. It doesn't have to be anything complicated—this is just a simple tool to help you accomplish what you want out of life, not something else to get in your way.

First thing on your To-Do list: Make a To-Do list—the right way

A simple To-Do list can be very effective, as long as you understand the best way to make it work for you.

First, draw a line down a sheet of paper. Title the left column Must-Do and the right column Should-Do. But how can you tell the difference?

Here's a great Must-Do qualifying question: "Will it negatively affect my life or career if I don't get this done today?" If it doesn't, it isn't a Must-Do! If it isn't a Must-Do, then it's a Should-Do.

Asking a great qualifying question will GREATLY reduce the number of items you Must-Do today. Everything else is a Should-Do.

Take your Must-Do list and prioritize it with the item you must complete first, then second and so on. Then DO THEM! It is that simple. If you take this clear, time-saving approach, you will complete your most important items first.

This next step is to prioritize your Should-Do list in the same manner. Start doing the first item on that list and so on. You'll find that the things of greatest importance to your life and career are getting done and that is your goal.

What happens when the To-Do list is done?

One huge benefit of having a daily To-Do list is this: When you've completed it, you can feel free to carry on with other important aspects of your life, like family, friends, hobbies, etc., without the burden of thinking about things that didn't happen that day. It gives you the freedom to "be in the moment" for the other valuable and important areas of your life.

Lesson: Time is not your enemy

Now you know one way that you CAN complete everything that you wanted each day. Plus, you are building a habit of success by attaining your goals, one by one, on a daily basis.

Every streak starts with accomplishing "one in a row!"

Door Opener

How often do you create a to-do list? Make it a habit to write your list out every day before you go to bed. This will give you your road map for the next morning.

Chapter 11

"BUSY"
The time pursuit!

The word "busy" is overused. It becomes an excuse for saying I am not interested in coming, buying or helping.

Truly the word "busy" has been overused and it seems like it is everyone's middle name.

Why can't we just use "detained," "not interested," "on the way," "some other time" or blatantly "NO."

Did I say NO? Most people do not know how to say "no," and they think that "busy" sounds better and will not hurt someone's feelings.

I say, "Boo hoo." I would rather hear the word "no" than "I am just too busy," or "I am busy with my children" or "I am just too busy, that day, week, month."

In other words, they are too busy for business.

Are you stuck on busy -- or busy being stuck?

You may wonder how being stuck has anything to do with being busy. I think we can get in a slump when we hear the word "busy" from everyone. It paralyzes us from getting out the door.

I assure you that this has happened to me, and after I heard this word time and time again I felt that I did not know what the right time was to call or contact anyone.

In fact, it stopped me dead in my tracks. It also made it hard for me to have a fast bounce-back ability.

Battling back against busy is not busy-work.

It wasn't until I had coffee with a wonderful mentor who said to me, "Ignore that word. It is an excuse." She said sometimes when people use the word "busy" they have a fear and we have to overcome it or just plain move on. Don't chase the business.

When was the last time you told someone you were "busy?"

When did you hear it last and felt let down or unsure of what the real circumstances were?

Remember – if you are honest with people, your credibility jumps up. The truth trumps excuses.

If you say you are busy time and time again, people feel you are always leading them on.

If you do pursue the "busy" word, why not ask questions that identify whether there is an interest in your product or service? Such as:

"I know you are busy. When would be a better time for me to call?"

"I know you are busy. Which is better for us to get together, day or evening?" Then, control the day and the time.

"I would love your opinion of our products or service, when are the best times to call?"

Don't consider "busy" a "no," and pursue your objective!

Door Opener

When you say you're busy, do you really mean no? How do you react when others offer being busy as an excuse? What strategies can you use to get past "busy" and achieve a yes?

_____

_____

_____

_____

_____

_____

_____

_____

_____

_____

_____

_____

_____

_____

_____

_____

_____

_____

_____

_____

_____

_____

_____

_____

5 Time Thieves

What's stealing your time—and profits? It just might be one of these 5 culprits.

1. **E-mail.**
   The ultimate time sponge. Schedule time to reply 2 or 3 times a day and encourage telephone calls.

2. **You.**
   You're burdened by tasks that make no money. Pass those functions to someone else. It's worth paying for, so you can do your real job.

3. **Your planner.**
   Use a day planner. Plan your day, hour-by-hour. Each scheduled item avoids procrastination and is a goal to get through business so you can get down to business. Maybe even a weekly plan sheet to develop your week. Color code so you can plan for business appointments, power hours in your office, errands for family or self and time for family, you and date nights.

4. **Your butt.**
   Get off it. Walk. Exercise. Eat and drink correctly. You'll find that the hours you feel most energized will grow, making time more efficient.

5. **Others.**
   You love them, but control their access to you (unless, of course, they are working for you!). When someone calls and the time is flying by and you want to cut the conversation, (if you work out of the house, go ring the door bell) ~ Got to go!

Door Opener

Where do you see yourself wasting time? What are you
going to do to change?

Dream and Think Big

You never know when a challenge can turn into an opportunity. I'd like to relate a personal story of mine that turned into a life-lesson for both my daughter and myself.

In early September of 1995, my daughter, Laura, came home from school excited about an assignment for her 8th grade math class.

"Mom," she said, "our math assignment for the semester is to run a business. What should I do?"

I knew that she needed something fun to last the semester. I was then in the insurance business, not something appropriate for her assignment. We talked it over all evening and finally I said, "Let's sleep on it and we can discuss it when you come home tomorrow afternoon."

Business is about people engaging other people.

I really had no idea what to suggest, but was hoping inspiration would come at the chamber of commerce networking function the next day. At the event, I was talking with several people when a woman approached me.

"Where did you get your awesome shoes?" she asked.

Her compliment floored me and we started talking. I told her about my commercial insurance agency and she told me her name was Kate and that she was a sales director for a direct marketing cosmetic company.

I admitted to knowing nothing about the company, although I had received some samples a few months earlier. She invited me to a special guest event so I could learn more about the company and meet some other great women.

This turned out to be the perfect answer, both for Laura's project and for me. Laura was very excited, and I started my direct-selling business alongside my insurance business that October.

What an amazing journey it was for both Laura and me. As I learned the business, she was incredibly helpful, working for me in my office doing the computer work, cleaning the cosmetic mirrors and packing my bags for the events. She also helped me make up holiday gift baskets and assisted with the open house gatherings.

I paid Laura $6 an hour. Half went to her and half went in her savings for college. As she saw her bank account starting to grow she was always encouraging me to get out the door and sell. I was so proud to see her take charge of the paper work and keep the office in order.

Laura's project for school ended up a huge success. We had the girls over before a dance and she did everyone's makeup and taught them the importance of good skin care. She took things to school for the girls to try and we set up mother/daughter events.

Not only was this a wonderful lesson in being an entrepreneur, but it also gave her a sense of worth and involvement in the bigger picture as our business unfolded.

Rewards are often priceless.

Perhaps the best moment of all was handing her a $3500 check at the end of her senior year – the money we'd been saving throughout her years working for me. The savings provided her with ample spending money for college, and was concrete evidence of her hard work and dedication.

Yet even more long-lasting than the monetary rewards were the life lessons she acquired. The company I represented taught me to fail forward, and I instilled that in her. You see, Laura was an extraordinary athlete, and I feel because of this project she learned to have a goal, be committed, have perseverance and always strive to be the best.

Laura was a pole vaulter and track star in high school. She took the tools we learned and pushed to better herself, reaching #2 in Western Massachusetts in vaulting when she graduated and the top ten in all of New England. She attended UNC at Chapel Hill, NC, made the Olympic trials for vaulting and also became a cosmetic consultant when she turned 18. She was chosen by the company to represent their young women's skin care line to test market new products. This was based on her goals, knowledge and skills.

Why is this story important to getting out the door or being stuck? If you have a small business, why not engage your children in the business? The life skills are invaluable. Working together builds a bond between you and gives your children a sense of responsibility. Your child can take pride in being part of your business and part of your successes.

Door Opener

What is it you can do to engage a family member to feel part of what you do? How can they help to keep you moving forward and also getting unstuck? Talk to your family members. Their input may surprise you.

_____

_____

_____

_____

_____

_____

_____

_____

_____

_____

_____

_____

_____

_____

_____

_____

_____

_____

_____

_____

_____

_____

_____

_____

Moving Forward—and Not In "Just Any Direction"
By Nicki Schuh

Do you ever feel like you're a gyroscope spinning around and around? You're expending a lot of energy and momentum but you still get nowhere--no forward progress. I call it "spiraling." Not always out of control, but just going nowhere! Not making decisions or not knowing which direction to take.

Stop the Spiraling!

First—stop, breathe, clear your mind. Look at your goals and determine what you can do TODAY that will help meet your goals. Clear your mind of all the clutter—all the "should dos," the negative thoughts or self-doubts, the priorities set by others. Take a walk, exercise, meditate. Figure out what works best for you.

Yes, you can do any number of things and probably have, but are you really progressing on your goals and implementing actions to achieve them? Stop the aimless spinning in one place—move in a direction—take a stand—make forward progress.

Get Strategic in Your Thoughts and Direction

I was once told by a business coach to write the word "NO" in big letters on a piece of paper, then put it in my business portfolio on top of my calendar. Then, pull it out every time I start to put something on my calendar or add to my to-do list. Use it often! As entrepreneurs we have a tendency to think (and do) several things at once, which causes us to become "diffused" like a light source, spreading out in many directions.

Second—form a business advisory group of three to five people who you believe have a high degree of strategic thought and you respect for their business acumen. (Make sure you like them as "people," as well!) This group of people becomes your advisors and should guide you in clarity of vision, mission, strategic direction and, ultimately, measures of success. Or join a Mastermind or similarly committed group that assists in direction setting and problem solving.

Be Accountable for Your Own Success!

Take charge of your destiny—have a plan, work the plan, adjust when needed, and celebrate the successes. No plan is perfect, but continuing to improve your ability to use the planning process, set direction and hold yourself accountable for the essence of the plan **(with implementable strategies and tactics)** feels powerful and leaves you poised for success.

If you find yourself slipping, hire a business coach. We all have distinct capabilities, and sometimes we need a coach to hold us accountable, point out our inconsistencies and keep us honest. Their skill is to help us be the BEST we can be. Goals, time lines and key performance indicators should be the essences of what you discuss each time you meet or talk by phone. Be open to their coaching and let them do their work. Their coaching techniques are successful only if (a) there is a defined set of goals, (b) we remain honest about progress or lack thereof, and (c) we utilize their expertise to keep our laser-like focus.

Chapter 14

Door Opener

What techniques work best for you? Who do you turn to for advice to get (and keep) you out of that spiral?

_____

_____

_____

_____

_____

_____

_____

_____

_____

_____

_____

_____

_____

_____

_____

_____

_____

_____

_____

_____

_____

_____

_____

Chapter 15

Even Superheroes Need Sidekicks
by Libby Kozak

Doing everything yourself is rarely efficient, or even effective. Whether you're a superhero or a businessperson, finding the right backup can make it even easier to be the success you're meant to be.

If you're just starting out or money is tight, paying someone to help you may seem impractical. But when you stop and think about how many billable or income-producing hours you have in a day or a week, it's more sensible than you think.

Assemble Your Own Justice League

Review your current to-do list. What tasks recur but don't get done? Which tasks are best done by someone else? Which tasks get in the way of your getting out the door and getting things done? Those are the tasks best delegated to your support team.

The amount of help and kind of assistance that you need may involve your hiring more than one person, each with specific tasks. Start by finding an assistant to manage business-related issues. The right candidate will be able to work independently once you've clearly communicated responsibilities and expectations.

Additionally, you might hire one person to clean your house, another to maintain the lawn and someone else to help with the children. Targeted task delegation allows you to pay the right price for each skill set and increase the likelihood that everything gets done on time and on budget.

Depending on the skill set you require, you may be able to find affordable help easily. Think outside the box – students and stay-home parents may have some under-utilized skills that will help your business thrive. That way you'll have the backup you need so you can get out the door and be super.

Get Some Help Already and Get Out the Door

Identifying tasks to off load and finding the right people for the job will give you the time and energy to focus on what you do best.

Can you do it all yourself? Absolutely. Is that the best way to spend your time and build your business? Absolutely not. Your goal is to build your business. Support staff makes it easier to do your job. Absolutely!

It's much easier to be a superhero when a strong, talented team has your back.

Chapter 15

Door Opener

Identify tasks you need to let go of so you can move forward. Who are you hiring today to simplify your life and let you focus on what you do best to build your business?

Chapter 16

Inspiration is an Inside Job
By Susan Carson, Ph.D.

How do you find the spark within you that will set off the fire needed to reach your dream?

When I met Jean many years ago, she was so inspirational and charged up about her direct selling business, I had no choice but to climb on board. I was, after all, a successful executive recruiter and I love people -- so how could I fail?

Little did I know then that you can observe someone else's energy and maybe borrow a bit, but ultimately you have to find your own energy and inspiration, so you can continually stoke it and let it grow. While it took years to learn this lesson, it has enabled me to help others uncover their own inner spark.

The Answer is Within You

Like me, you've probably attended many management/self-help seminars, the ones where they promise you everything from the "perfect" organizing system to the "secret of life" to essentials on managing your staff. We've all done it – seeking and searching for all the answers in others, whether self-proclaimed gurus or established professionals.

Through my coaching training I have learned that, in reality, it all comes down to me. Everything I need to be successful is within me. My authentic self provides my inspiration and my energy to be present, to glorify in the world and all its gifts, and to give back. Now I am ready to "hear" all great wisdom out there. To take what I want, leave the rest, and share the best.

Recently Jean and I really reconnected and I began coaching her. What a funny expression, "I coached her." Actually, I have learned so much from our conversations. I have watched her grow and evolve even more than I thought possible – for I thought she had it all when we first met.

Listen to Yourself

I ask people: Have you wondered why even though you have dreams and goals you just don't move – or if you do move, all you move is backwards? Have you ever wondered why you seem to sabotage yourself even though you know "the right way" and listen to the "right people?"

Chapter 16

The truth is that you do know the right way. And that deep down inside of each of us we have the truth; we have the authenticity we were born with. But over the years, so much stuff has been piled on top of our truth that we cannot even see it. Just as when we were children, we had the ability to overcome the severest challenge – that of changing from a mewling, pooping, eating machine to an upright, walking, talking human being – we still have that ability within us.

I remember when I was 42 and newly pregnant for the first time and scared out of my mind. The doctor sent me for an ultrasound at about three weeks of pregnancy. All the ultrasound showed us of our evolving child was a flashing light. That is the gift in all of us, the seat of our inspiration, our hearts, our souls, our passions -- and it still is flashing.

All we have to do is uncover it and let it light up the world.

Chapter 16

Door Opener

What inspires you? What are you grateful for? What makes you unique and special? Celebrate your inner spark by stepping up, stepping out and living an inspiring life.

_____

_____

_____

_____

_____

_____

_____

_____

_____

_____

_____

_____

_____

_____

_____

_____

_____

_____

_____

_____

_____

_____

Find Your Focus
By Kristen Schoch

There are many definitions of focus – from a central idea to a clear optical image to a specific geometrical point. Whether physical or conceptual, this focus is our goal -- what we hope to achieve and accomplish. To be successful, in business or in our personal lives, we must first identify our goal, then pursue it with focus.

What are your goals? Starting your own business, buying your dream house, paying for college tuition, or perhaps buying those cute new shoes? Whatever you are pursuing, you must first understand what you want, identify what is required to get there, create a plan to achieve your goal, and be persistent until you succeed.

Belief is the foundation of focus.

There is an expression, "If you can dream it, you can achieve it." When you have real focus, you not only have a dream, but you have passion and a plan behind it to make it happen. Do you believe you can achieve your dreams? I certainly do!

I've been told that some view success this way:

When in fact, the line looks a lot more like…

We'd like to think that life is the easy path above. However, the second image not only is more realistic, but is more in line with a strong sense of focus. There are so many distractions out there that it is only by creating a strong plan and revisiting it frequently that we can continue to move in the right direction. Your focus will help you prioritize and regroup when the unexpected happens.

Focus is the foundation of success.

Be deliberate in your choices. Be relentless in pursuing your goal. Re-evaluate when necessary, and don't be afraid to adjust your plans. If something's not working, fix it.People with focus prosper. Without focus they flounder. Identify your goals, visualize your success, and start today working towards success.

Chapter 17

Door Opener

Identify where you want to go – personally and professionally. Are you heading in the right direction or do you need to shift your focus?

_____

_____

_____

_____

_____

_____

_____

_____

_____

_____

_____

_____

_____

_____

_____

_____

_____

_____

_____

_____

_____

_____

_____

Diamonds on the Ground

I will never forget when I started working for an insurance agency in New Jersey. Young, full of piss and vinegar (as my mother would say) and eager to go out and sell. I was unstoppable (at least I thought I was).

I wanted so much to be in sales, and in the 70s there just were not a lot of women in the commercial insurance business. I worked as an administrative assistant, receptionist, junior underwriter, customer service representative and finally worked in an agency where they gave me an opportunity to get my license to sell property and casualty insurance.

I was so excited and thought I was on my way to selling, but my boss had other things in mind. He wanted me to service accounts already written. I felt I was back at the beginning. It did not make me happy, and I decided to look for another job. Off I went from agency to agency with no success.

The diamonds are there for all of us.

Finally, I was given a lead to a local agency looking for new sales associates. I went to this local agency and met with the owner. He said, "I will give you this job and pay you $300 a week for 3 months. After that you are on straight commission."

It scared me to death, when next he said, "It is so simple, and most people never get it. There are two keys to success. When you learn these, success will follow." He asked me to get a pen and paper out and write these valuable lessons down. First he said, "All you need to do is pick up the diamonds lying on the ground." At this point I wasn't sure this was making much sense, but I realized that he knew what he was doing since he owned a multi-million dollar agency.

Listening is key.

I listened intently and started writing notes as he spoke. He explained that most never even see the diamonds. He went on to explain that the diamonds are the relationships we build, the attitude we have, the care and follow-up that we do that will bring us the first key to success. He went on to say that this will take years to learn but the credibility and integrity we build will be invaluable.

As for the second key to success, this comes from all we do and all the people we help along the way. When we work smart and earn our way, the second key is to pass it on to others, mentor and help them grow.

Chapter 18

At first it made no sense to me, but after working with him, watching how he took great pride in making his customers feel important and making sure to do the proper follow-up and customer care it all started to come together. He was the master of building strong relationships.

Relationship building is essential.

I will never forget his words. They made me realize how important it was to work with business associates and prospects to build solid business relationships. Work with my customers by treating them with respect and listen. Also asking for referrals and looking for the hidden diamonds in all I did.

I see so many people chasing the business. Never caring about others, looking for connections and never listening to what others need. The old adage like I said before is so true – "When you help and reach out to others, it will come back ten-fold."

Chapter 18

Door Opener

Are you chasing the business, always searching and feeling stressed, or are you picking up the diamonds that are shining right in front of you?

_____

_____

_____

_____

_____

_____

_____

_____

_____

_____

_____

_____

_____

_____

_____

_____

_____

_____

_____

_____

Conclusion
Get back to the basics.
Get Up, Get Dressed and Get Out the Door

TODAY!

You Know You're an Achiever if...

- ▌ You attract people because of the person you are.
- ▌ Your self-view and attitude create who you are -- you are not shaped by others.
- ▌ You don't give up on challenges -- you are committed to your goals.
- ▌ You expect success, and blame no one else for lack of success or failure.
- ▌ You bring value to each person in your network.
- ▌ You feel that your only competition is yourself.
- ▌ Your best friends and colleagues are achievers.
- ▌ Your worst enemies are forgotten, if not forgiven.

I hope you enjoyed this book. Keep the "door openers" in mind.

List your strengths and achievements, then **celebrate!**

Contributors

Susan Carson, Ph.D.
Smart Leadership Coaching
susan@smartleadershipcoaching.com
www.smartleadershipcoaching.com
817-742-0380

Executive Coach, Educator, Speaker, Scientist, Founder Smart Leadership Coaching, Developer of Catalyst for Results Program.

Phil Gafka, CBC
LEAP Associates, Inc.
phil@leapassociates.us
www.leapassociates.com
847-212-4903

Certified Business Coach, Founder and Principal of LEAP Associates, Inc., (Leadership for Entrepreneurs and Professionals), an industry leading, executive coaching and business development firm.

Libby Kozak
Professional Impressions
ElizKozak@gmail.com
413-244-2765

Professional writing and proofreading including newsletters and promotional materials. Helping you look good online, in print and in person.

Kristen Lewandowski Schoch
Wellness Consultant and Leader
kristen.schoch@yahoo.com
www.myalphay.com/schoch
443-803-1845

Educating individuals and companies on the importance of wellness. Teaching with unique healthy products, you can attain the best immunity, vitality and energy.

Beverly McKeen

Professional Speaker/Author
beverly@beverlymckeen.com
www.beverlymckeen.com
847-902-2844

Whether you are looking for a practical message for your event or uplifting entertainment, Beverly's message will inspire audiences to take action on their dreams.

Laura Risi

Sweet Hysteria
laura@sweethysteria.com
www.sweethysteria.com
919-200-3105

Scrumptious candies, speciality "Whoopie Pies" made with flavorful combinations designed with the customer in mind, shipped around the country.

Nicki Schuh

NLS Enterprises
nlschuh@comcast.net
www.charitycards.com
847-772-8662

Using "laser-like focus and direction setting" to assist her clients in growing their businesses and achieving success in their lives.

Tim Schoch

Versatile Writer and Marketing Communication Professional
timschoch@gmail.com
www.linkedin.com/in/timschoch

Novelist, magazine writer, sports blogger, ghostwriter, and mentor to dozens of young writers. He's worked on projects from Broadway theater and television publicity to grassroots communication for salespeople across a number of major industries.

Resources

These organizations and websites have helped me continually improve my business growth.

BNI International
www.bni.com/ BNI International - Business Networking and Referrals, the world's largest business networking organization.

eWomen Network
www.ewomennetwork.com/
Join over 2000 outstanding professional women.

LinkedIn
www.linkedin.com/
Manage your professional identity. Build and engage with your professional network. Access knowledge, insights and opportunities.

Meetup
www.meetup.com/
Helps groups of people with shared interests plan meetings and form offline clubs in local communities around the world.

Jeffrey Gitomer
www.gitomer.com/
Sales training books and seminars - sales techniques to motivate your salesforce.

John Maxwell
www.johnmaxwellonleadership.com/
John C Maxwell's personal blog, sharing his thoughts on all aspects of leadership and influence.

SUCCESS Magazine
www.success.com/
Your leading source for news and information for the entrepreneur, small business, and home-based business owner.

Toastmasters International
www.toastmasters.org/
Non-profit organization developing public speaking and leadership skills through practice and feedback in local clubs since 1924.

Twitter
www.twitter.com/
Instantly connect to what's most important to you. Follow your friends, experts, favorite celebrities, and breaking news.

U.S. Chamber of Commerce
www.uschamber.com/
A business federation representing companies, business associations, state and local chambers in the U.S.

About the Author

Combining enthusiasm with an energetic speaking style, Jean MacDonald creates a spark of inspiration wherever she presents. She conveys her messages with the power, passion and presence proven to motivate others to achieve their goals and dreams. Jean knows that attitude is 95 percent of the winning score, and this is reflected in how she relates to her audience and inspires them to be the best they can be. Jean is a true leader – motivating, educating and empowering – yet a woman who speaks from the heart with a touch of humility. Having risen through the ranks in the challenging commercial insurance industry while raising and supporting three children single-handedly, Jean openly shares her life lessons with others.

Following a 10-year career building a multimillion dollar insurance agency as a rare female executive in the field, Jean's journey took a surprising turn when her daughter approached her for help with a high school class project. They needed to "run a business" – and decided to try a direct-selling cosmetics venture. What began as a homework assignment more than eighteen years ago has shaped Jean into the leader she is today.

Today, Jean is one of 6 founding members for the North American launch of a 52 year old wellness company, Alphay Global. She is helping others develop their skills and talents to build worldwide in the next 5 years. Jean currently serves on the women's board of directors, for Rainbows (helping kids through life storms). She and her husband, Greg, divide their time between the midwest and east coast She has two sons, a daughter and two granddaughters.

Her next book, to be released soon, is "Stick Your Neck Out." Now that you have gotten out the door and back to the basics, get off your bottom to get to the top.

The Vision of Today is the Abundance of Tomorrow!

Jean MacDonald

Hire Jean for your next event, seminar or conference. She'll share her secrets for networking that connects the dots, Vision Casting that conveys just the right message, and opening doors to new possibilities.

GUIDING KIDS THROUGH LIFE'S STORMS

A portion of the proceeds from this book will be donated to
Rainbows International
a grief support organization for children.